Copyright © by Harcourt, Inc.

All rights reserved. No part of this publication may be reproduced or transmitted in any form or by any means, electronic or mechanical, including photocopy, recording, or any information storage and retrieval system, without permission in writing from the publisher.

Requests for permission to make copies of any part of the work should be addressed to School Permissions and Copyrights, Harcourt, Inc., 6277 Sea Harbor Drive, Orlando, Florida 32887-6777. Fax: 407-345-2418.

HARCOURT and the Harcourt Logo are trademarks of Harcourt, Inc., registered in the United States of America and/or other jurisdictions.

Printed in Hong Kong

ISBN-13: 978-0-15-352742-5
ISBN-10: 0-15-352742-0

If you have received these materials as examination copies free of charge, Harcourt School Publishers retains title to the materials and they may not be resold. Resale of examination copies is strictly prohibited and is illegal.

Possession of this publication in print format does not entitle users to convert this publication, or any portion of it, into electronic format.

7 8 9 10   985   11 10 09 08

Visit *The Learning Site!* www.harcourtschool.com

Everybody Plays!

Who plays games? Kids do. Grown-ups do. All around the world, people play games. What kind of games do you play? Maybe you like sitting games. Maybe you like moving games. Maybe you like both.

Ready, Set, Go!

Camel racing is an old game. It is more than 1,000 years old. Riders sit on camels. They race up to 5 miles. Some camels can go as fast as cars on city streets! Camel races are held in Africa, India, and southwestern Asia.

Kids from many cultures play these games. Look at this list.

- Board games
- Guessing games
- Ball games
- Racing and chasing games
- Hiding games

In Kenya, people play mancala. ▼

Running Games

Try these games from other lands.

Make one long line to play Dragon Tail. The first person is the dragon's head. This person tries to catch the last person, who is the tail.

▼ Dragon Tail

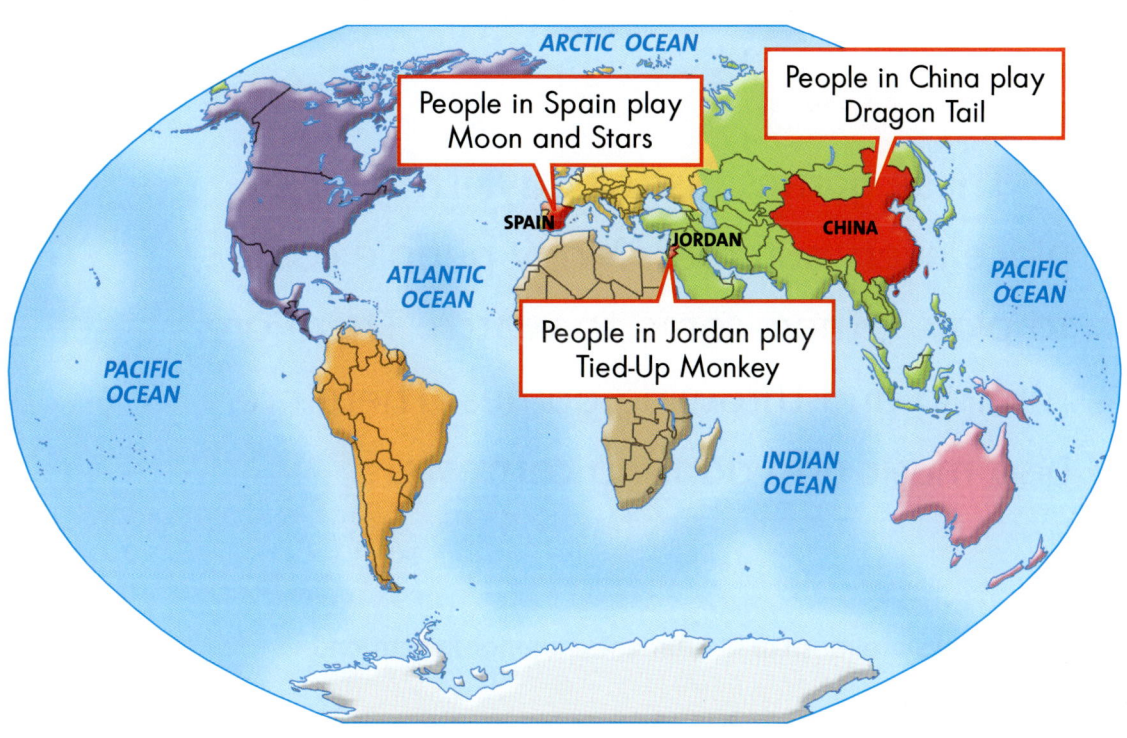

Children play Moon and Stars under a tree. The "Moon" tries to catch the "Stars". The Moon must keep one foot in the tree's shadow. Stars can run anywhere!

Another game is Tied-Up Monkey. One player is the Monkey. Other players put their shoes under a tree. Then they try to grab them back. The Monkey tries to tag them!

Scotland's Highland Games

These games last all day. They take place every summer. Many people come to play. Others come to watch. There are running and throwing games. There are also music and dancing contests.

▼ Bagpipes are musical instruments popular in Scotland.

▲ There are many dancing contests.

Games are held all over Scotland. Some events are for children. Girls and boys run races. Teams of children play tug-of-war.

Children have fun. They learn about the history of their country.

Think and Respond

1. Name three kinds of games.
2. How are Moon and Stars and Tied-Up Monkey alike?
3. What happens at the Highland Games?
4. Why do children all over the world like to play games?

Activity

Work with a group to play a game from this book.

Photo Credits
Front Cover STR/AFP/Getty Images; 2 Jodi Cobb/National Geographic Image Collection; 3 Margaret Courtney-Clarke/Corbis; 6 Steve Vidler/SuperStock; 7 Steve Vidler/SuperStock.

Illustration Credits
4 Paul Sharp; 5 Mapquest